Christoph S.
dump dumb Trump
Variations on a dangerous moron

AF282433

Christoph S.

dump dumb Trump

Variations on a dangerous moron. Here we ask ourselves: "How many variations of "dump dumb Trump" can we create?"

Impressum

Bibliografische Information der Deutschen Nationalbibliothek: Die Deutsche Nationalbibliothek verzeichnet diese Publikation in der Deutschen Nationalbibliografie; detaillierte bibliografische Daten sind im Internet über http://dnb.dnb.de abrufbar.

Verlag: BoD · Books on Demand GmbH, Überseering 33, 22297 Hamburg, bod@bod.de

Druck: Libri Plureos GmbH, Friedensallee 273, 22763 Hamburg

ISBN: 978-3-8192-6362-0

Index

CHAPTER 1: THE EASY ONES

Synonym-based & Similar Verbs

Ditch ditch Trump
Drop drop Trump
Dump ditch Trump
Toss toss Trump
Boot boot Trump
Flush flush Trump
Scrap scrap Trump
Kick kick Trump
Chop chop Trump
Bin bin Trump
Expel expel Trump
Fire fire Trump
Reject reject Trump
Bounce bounce Trump
Oust oust Trump
Unload unload Trump
Shed shed Trump
Purge purge Trump
Abandon abandon Trump
Dismiss dismiss Trump
Turf turf Trump
Can can Trump

Evict evict Trump
Relieve relieve Trump
Heave-ho Trump
Downsize Trump
Trump, you're terminated
Vote out Trump

Alliterative / Rhyming / Repetition

Dump Drumpf Trump
Thump Trump Dump
Bump dump Trump
Jump Trump dump
Slump Trump dump
Grump Trump dump
Clump dump Trump
Plump Trump dump
Stump dump Trump
Hump dump Trump
Lump dump Trump
Crump dump Trump
Grump grump Trump
Thump thump Trump
Whomp whomp Trump
Gump dump Trump
Sump sump Trump
Pump dump Trump
Rump bump Trump
Bloop bloop Trump
Boop boop Trump
Bleep bleep Trump
Yup yup dump Trump
Dump Trump Jump
Jump Jump, Dump Trump

Bump the Trump
Chump Trump Dump
Stomp stomp Trump
Clomp clomp Trump
Honk honk Trump**

Wordplay / Satirical / Puns

Trump the Dump
Make Trump Dump Again
Orange you gonna dump Trump?
Dump Tower Power
Bigly Dump Trump
Covfefe the Dump Trump
MAGA? More like DUMPGA!
Drain the Swamp, Dump the Trump
No Rump for Trump
Bye Don Dump
Make America Dump Again
Dump the Don
Time's up, Trump
Unpresident Trump
No More Trump Cards
End the Trump Show
Dump the Apprentice
Fire the Liar
No Trumper Tantrums
The Dump Stops Here
Trump? I barely knew 'em!
Orange Eviction Notice
Keep Calm and Dump Trump
ByeDon 2.0
The Art of the Dump
You're Fired, Again

Exit Don, Stage Left
Drain Trump, Not the Swamp
From MAGA to Trash Baga
Dumpster Don

Meme Vibes

Dumpity Dump Trump
Dumpsterfire Don
Dumpy Mc Trumpface
Operation Orange Toss
Dumpster Supreme
No Cap Dump Trump
Bye Felicia: Trump Edition
Yeet the Cheeto
Ain't No Trumpo
Trashbag Donnie
Cheeto Get Out-o
Dumpzilla vs Democracy
The Fall of Trumpire
The Orange Has Spoiled
Bye Bye Big Lie
Faux News? Dump the Muse.
Bad Wig Energy: Dump It
From Trump to Chump
The Only Wall We Need: Between Us and Trump
Ye Olde Don Dump

Clever Wordplay & Satire

Dump the dumb Trump before he turns logic into landfill.

Don't just debate — dump the dumb Trump and detour the drama.

We tried facts, we tried patience — now it's time to dump dumb Trump.

Dump the dumb Trump and disinfect the democracy.

From chaos to cringe, let's finally dump the dumb Trump binge.

Aggressive / Protest-Style

Dump the dumb Trump and take the wheel back from the wreck.

We've had enough lies, hate, and grift — dump dumb Trump and uplift.

Don't let the dumb Trump thump your rights — dump him tonight.

He's the chaos king in a clown crown — time to dump dumb Trump down.

Dump dumb Trump like yesterday's trash -— 'cause democracy's worth more than cash.

Rhythmic, Poetic, or Spoken Word Vibes

When fear leads and facts flee, we dump dumb Trump to set minds free.

We've seen the tweets, the tantrums, the spin — now dump dumb Trump and begin again.

No more walls, no more stunts — dump the dumb Trump and lift the fronts.

He stumbles through truths and dances with doom — time to dump dumb Trump from the room.

Dump dumb Trump like expired noise — we're done being pawns in his ploy.

Funny / Meme-Worthy

Dump the dumb Trump before he turns the White House into a weird reality show reunion.

He's the human version of a broken pop-up ad — dump dumb Trump and clear the cache.

Dump dumb Trump like you would an MLM pitch from your cousin.

Like expired cheese on a hot sidewalk — dump dumb Trump before he stinks up the century.

He's got more drama than a soap opera villain — dump the dumb Trump and change the channel.

CHAPTER 2: FIFTY EXTENDED SENTENCES BASED ON "DUMP DUMB TRUMP"

1. Dump the dumb Trump before his next tantrum tanks the truth.

2. We're done with the lies, the grift, the game — it's time to dump dumb Trump and reclaim the name.

3. Dump dumb Trump like bad Wi-Fi on a Monday Zoom call.

4. Like a pop-up ad from 2003, it's time to dump the dumb Trump permanently.

5. Dump the dumb Trump before he speed-runs democracy into disaster.

6. If ignorance is bliss, then dumb Trump's living in Disneyland — let's dump him already.

7. Dump dumb Trump like you would a group text from your ex's MLM.

8. The world needs healing, not trolling — dump the dumb Trump and start rolling.

9. We dumped dial-up — now let's dump dumb Trump too.

10. Truth doesn't trend in Trumpworld — so dump the dumb before we're all gaslit into oblivion.

11. Dump the dumb Trump before irony collapses from exhaustion.

12. The brain drain is real — dump dumb Trump before it spreads.

13. He's like a glitch in democracy's mainframe — dump dumb Trump and reboot.

14. The walls he promised? Still not built. Dump dumb Trump for results, not rants.

15. He's the boss of blame and the prince of pettiness — dump dumb Trump and grow up.

16. If BS were energy, dumb Trump could power the grid — but dump him anyway.

17. He treats facts like toys — time to dump dumb Trump and speak like adults.

18. It's not politics, it's performance art — dump dumb Trump before Act 3 begins.

19. He says he's a genius, but spells like a meme — dump the dumb Trump and redeem the dream.

20. Dump dumb Trump like expired milk on a summer day.

21. He's got more scandals than socks — dump dumb Trump and let the grown-ups talk.

22. He built a brand on bluster — now dump dumb Trump and restore the roster.

23. Dump the dumb Trump like you would a haunted Roomba.

24. We dumped Blockbuster. We dumped Myspace. Now let's dump dumb Trump.

25. Every sentence from him is a word salad with rage dressing — dump dumb Trump.

26. Democracy isn't a reality show — dump dumb Trump and cancel the season.

27. If narcissism were a sport, Trump's the undefeated champ — dump him before the next match.

28. We're not tired of winning — we're tired of whining. Dump dumb Trump.

29. Dumb Trump says "many people are saying" — we say "dump him today."

30. Let's build bridges, not echo chambers — dump the dumb Trump and move forward.

31. We need nuance, not nonsense — dump dumb Trump now.

32. Dump dumb Trump before the tweetstorm turns into a constitutional crisis.

33. Dump him like fake crypto — flashy, empty, and draining your future.

34. He'd sell the country for a compliment — dump dumb Trump.

35. Like a broken clock that screams, dump dumb Trump and silence the noise.

36. Dump the dumb Trump — facts are not negotiable.

37. He golfs while the world burns — dump dumb Trump and pass the torch.

38. The only thing he builds is tension — dump dumb Trump and breathe again.

39. Dump the dumb Trump — your grandkids will thank you.

40. Leadership takes more than tweets — dump dumb Trump and raise the standard.

41. Dump dumb Trump like your playlist dumped that one cringy song.

42. He's the algorithm of anger — dump dumb Trump and reset the feed.

43. The only wall he built was between people — dump him and tear it down.

44. History is watching — it's time to dump dumb Trump and write better chapters.

45. There's no "again" in this mess — dump dumb Trump and start anew.

46. You don't need a stable genius, just a stable leader — dump dumb Trump.

47. Dump the dumb Trump before the punchline becomes policy.

48. Time to trade the circus for service — dump dumb Trump.

49. He yells louder than he leads — dump dumb Trump and bring back dignity.

50. We've outgrown the cult of personality — dump dumb Trump and embrace reality.

CHAPTER 3: GROK GIVES 206 RE-SULTS LIKE THEY WERE MADE WITH PYTHON

Abandon bumbling Trump, a hazard to reason.
Abandon clueless Trump, a hazard to the future.
Abandon daft Trump, endangering the nation.
Abandon dense Trump, faltering in his lies.
Abandon dim Trump, stumbling through his role.
Abandon erratic Trump, tripping over truth.
Abandon feckless Trump, wrecking every chance.
Abandon foolish Trump, a parody of power.
Abandon goofy Trump, chasing foolish schemes.
Abandon hapless Trump, stumbling through chaos.
Abandon mindless Trump, tripping on his words.
Abandon reckless Trump, a danger to progress.
Abandon scatterbrained Trump, a leader without focus.
Abandon silly Trump, chasing empty promises.
Abandon witless Trump, faltering under pressure.
Cast off bumbling Trump, lost in his own world.
Cast off clueless Trump, tripping on his pride.
Cast off daft Trump, tripping over his ego.
Cast off dense Trump, wrecking every plan.
Cast off dim Trump, a danger to democracy.
Cast off erratic Trump, lost in his own confusion.
Cast off feckless Trump, lost in his own hype.
Cast off foolish Trump, wrecking every hope.
Cast off goofy Trump, chasing empty goals.
Cast off hapless Trump, faltering under scrutiny.
Cast off mindless Trump, a leader without sense.
Cast off reckless Trump, endangering all he leads.

Cast off scatterbrained Trump, a leader without merit.
Cast off silly Trump, chasing foolish dreams.
Cast off witless Trump, lost in his own mess.
Discard dim Trump, a parody of leadership.
Ditch bumbling Trump, a risk to stability.
Ditch clueless Trump, endangering all hope.
Ditch daft Trump, botching every chance.
Ditch dense Trump, floundering in chaos.
Ditch dim Trump, muddling every decision.
Ditch dopey Trump, botching every move.
Ditch erratic Trump, failing at every turn.
Ditch feckless Trump, whose policies falter and fade.
Ditch foolish Trump, a hazard to peace.
Ditch goofy Trump, a danger to stability.
Ditch hapless Trump, floundering in his role.
Ditch mindless Trump, a mockery of authority.
Ditch reckless Trump, fumbling through every debate.
Ditch scatterbrained Trump, faltering in every step.
Ditch silly Trump, floundering in his lies.
Ditch witless Trump, steering the nation to ruin.
Drop bumbling Trump, a leader without vision.
Drop clueless Trump, endangering all he touches.
Drop daft Trump, floundering in deep waters.
Drop dense Trump, stumbling through leadership.
Drop dim Trump, a burden on progress.
Drop erratic Trump, a hazard to sensible governance.
Drop feckless Trump, floundering in his own mess.
Drop foolish Trump, a foolish leader with reckless plans.
Drop goofy Trump, swaying with every breeze.
Drop hapless Trump, faltering in every choice.
Drop mindless Trump, endangering the nation's future.
Drop reckless Trump, stumbling through his term.
Drop scatterbrained Trump, lost in his own noise.
Drop silly Trump, a leader without a plan.

Drop witless Trump, stumbling through his lies.
Dump bumbling Trump, tripping on his own ego.
Dump clueless Trump, botching every policy.
Dump daft Trump, a liability in charge.
Dump dense Trump, a hazard to progress.
Dump dim Trump, a liability to all.
Dump dumb Trump, tripping on his own pride.
Dump erratic Trump, a mockery of governance.
Dump feckless Trump, a burden on the nation.
Dump foolish Trump, wrecking all he touches.
Dump goofy Trump, lost in his own rhetoric.
Dump hapless Trump, a clown in the spotlight.
Dump mindless Trump, bungling every critical choice.
Dump reckless Trump, a disaster in charge.
Dump scatterbrained Trump, a mockery of leadership.
Dump silly Trump, bungling critical moments.
Dump witless Trump, a blundering figure in chaos.
Eject bumbling Trump, a danger to the nation.
Eject clueless Trump, endangering the future.
Eject daft Trump, a risk to all progress.
Eject dense Trump, a parody of authority.
Eject dim Trump, faltering in his role.
Eject dimwit Trump, a clown in serious times.
Eject erratic Trump, wrecking progress with glee.
Eject feckless Trump, a burden on democracy.
Eject foolish Trump, tripping over his words.
Eject goofy Trump, endangering all with whims.
Eject hapless Trump, lost in his own lies.
Eject mindless Trump, a mockery of wisdom.
Eject reckless Trump, bungling every chance.
Eject scatterbrained Trump, bungling critical tasks.
Eject silly Trump, botching every opportunity.
Eject witless Trump, a risk to the nation.
Jettison bumbling Trump, a leader without a clue.

Jettison clueless Trump, stumbling over simple truths.
Jettison daft Trump, a leader in disarray.
Jettison dense Trump, a risk to progress.
Jettison dim Trump, a hazard to reason.
Jettison dull Trump, a hazard to the future.
Jettison erratic Trump, endangering the nation.
Jettison feckless Trump, faltering in his lies.
Jettison foolish Trump, stumbling through his role.
Jettison goofy Trump, tripping over truth.
Jettison hapless Trump, wrecking every chance.
Jettison mindless Trump, a parody of power.
Jettison reckless Trump, chasing foolish schemes.
Jettison scatterbrained Trump, stumbling through chaos.
Jettison silly Trump, tripping on his words.
Jettison witless Trump, a danger to progress.
Oust bumbling Trump, a leader without focus.
Oust clueless Trump, chasing empty promises.
Oust daft Trump, faltering under pressure.
Oust dense Trump, lost in his own world.
Oust dim Trump, tripping on his pride.
Oust erratic Trump, tripping over his ego.
Oust feckless Trump, wrecking every plan.
Oust foolish Trump, a danger to democracy.
Oust goofy Trump, lost in his own confusion.
Oust hapless Trump, lost in his own hype.
Oust mindless Trump, wrecking every hope.
Oust muddled Trump, chasing empty goals.
Oust reckless Trump, faltering under scrutiny.
Oust scatterbrained Trump, a leader without sense.
Oust silly Trump, endangering all he leads.
Oust witless Trump, a leader without merit.
Reject bumbling Trump, chasing foolish dreams.
Reject clueless Trump, lost in his own mess.
Reject daft Trump, a parody of leadership.

Reject dense Trump, a risk to stability.

Reject dim Trump, endangering all hope.

Reject dull Trump, botching every chance.

Reject erratic Trump, floundering in chaos.

Reject feckless Trump, muddling every decision.

Reject foolish Trump, botching every move.

Reject goofy Trump, failing at every turn.

Reject hapless Trump, whose policies falter and fade.

Reject mindless Trump, a hazard to peace.

Reject reckless Trump, a danger to stability.

Reject scatterbrained Trump, floundering in his role.

Reject silly Trump, a mockery of authority.

Reject witless Trump, fumbling through every debate.

Scrap blundering Trump, faltering in every step.

Scrap bumbling Trump, floundering in his lies.

Scrap clueless Trump, steering the nation to ruin.

Scrap daft Trump, a leader without vision.

Scrap dense Trump, endangering all he touches.

Scrap dim Trump, floundering in deep waters.

Scrap erratic Trump, stumbling through leadership.

Scrap feckless Trump, a burden on progress.

Scrap foolish Trump, a hazard to sensible governance.

Scrap goofy Trump, floundering in his own mess.

Scrap hapless Trump, a foolish leader with reckless plans.

Scrap mindless Trump, swaying with every breeze.

Scrap reckless Trump, faltering in every choice.

Scrap scatterbrained Trump, endangering the nation's future.

Scrap silly Trump, stumbling through his term.

Scrap witless Trump, lost in his own noise.

Shun brainless Trump, a leader without a plan.

Shun bumbling Trump, stumbling through his lies.

Shun clueless Trump, tripping on his own ego.

Shun daft Trump, botching every policy.

Shun dense Trump, a liability in charge.

Shun dim Trump, a hazard to progress.

Shun erratic Trump, a liability to all.

Shun feckless Trump, tripping on his own pride.

Shun foolish Trump, a mockery of governance.

Shun goofy Trump, a burden on the nation.

Shun hapless Trump, wrecking all he touches.

Shun mindless Trump, lost in his own rhetoric.

Shun reckless Trump, a clown in the spotlight.

Shun scatterbrained Trump, bungling every critical choice.

Shun silly Trump, a disaster in charge.

Shun witless Trump, a mockery of leadership.

Spurn bumbling Trump, bungling critical moments.

Spurn clueless Trump, a blundering figure in chaos.

Spurn daft Trump, a danger to the nation.

Spurn dense Trump, endangering the future.

Spurn dim Trump, a risk to all progress.

Spurn dimwit Trump, a parody of authority.

Spurn erratic Trump, faltering in his role.

Spurn feckless Trump, a clown in serious times.

Spurn foolish Trump, wrecking progress with glee.

Spurn goofy Trump, a burden on democracy.

Spurn hapless Trump, tripping over his words.

Spurn mindless Trump, endangering all with whims.

Spurn reckless Trump, lost in his own lies.

Spurn scatterbrained Trump, a mockery of wisdom.

Spurn silly Trump, bungling every chance.

Spurn witless Trump, bungling critical tasks.

Toss bumbling Trump, botching every opportunity.

Toss clueless Trump, a risk to the nation.

Toss daft Trump, a leader without a clue.

Toss dense Trump, stumbling over simple truths.

Toss dim Trump, a leader in disarray.

Toss erratic Trump, a risk to progress.

Toss feckless Trump, a hazard to reason.
Toss foolish Trump, a hazard to the future.
Toss goofy Trump, endangering the nation.
Toss hapless Trump, faltering in his lies.
Toss mindless Trump, stumbling through his role.
Toss muddled Trump, tripping over truth.
Toss reckless Trump, wrecking every chance.
Toss scatterbrained Trump, a parody of power.
Toss silly Trump, chasing foolish schemes.
Toss witless Trump, stumbling through chaos.

America deserves leaders, not clowns. `#ByeDon #DumpTheDumb #DumpTrump #EnoughIsEnough #MakeAmericaThinkAgain`

America deserves leaders, not clowns. `#NoMoreLies #TakeOutTheTrash #TimeForChange #TruthMatters #VoteThemOut`

Dumb isn't a policy. Dump Trump. `#ByeDon #DumpTheDumb #DumpTrump #EnoughIsEnough #MakeAmericaThinkAgain`

Dumb isn't a policy. Dump Trump. `#NoMoreLies #TakeOutTheTrash #TimeForChange #TruthMatters #VoteThemOut`

Dump dumb Trump. We've got better things to do. `#ByeDon #DumpTheDumb #DumpTrump #EnoughIsEnough #MakeAmericaThinkAgain`

Dump dumb Trump. We've got better things to do. `#NoMoreLies #TakeOutTheTrash #TimeForChange #TruthMatters #VoteThemOut`

Dump Trump like bad Wi-Fi. No signal, no service. `#ByeDon #DumpTheDumb #DumpTrump #EnoughIsEnough #MakeAmericaThinkAgain`

Dump Trump like bad Wi-Fi. No signal, no service. `#NoMoreLies #TakeOutTheTrash #TimeForChange #TruthMatters #VoteThemOut`

He tweets, we suffer. Time to dump dumb Trump. `#ByeDon #DumpTheDumb #DumpTrump #EnoughIsEnough #MakeAmericaThinkAgain`

He tweets, we suffer. Time to dump dumb Trump. #No-MoreLies #TakeOutTheTrash #TimeForChange #TruthMatters #VoteThemOut

Leadership isn't loud lies — dump dumb Trump. #Bye-Don #DumpTheDumb #DumpTrump #EnoughIsEnough #MakeAmericaThinkAgain

Leadership isn't loud lies — dump dumb Trump. #No-MoreLies #TakeOutTheTrash #TimeForChange #TruthMatters #VoteThemOut

Real patriots know when to say goodbye. #ByeDon #DumpTheDumb #DumpTrump #EnoughIsEnough #MakeAmericaThinkAgain

Real patriots know when to say goodbye. #NoMoreLies #TakeOutTheTrash #TimeForChange #TruthMatters #VoteThemOut

Still waiting on the 'greatness'? #ByeDon #DumpTheDumb #DumpTrump #EnoughIsEnough #MakeAmericaThink-Again

Still waiting on the 'greatness'? #NoMoreLies #Take-OutTheTrash #TimeForChange #TruthMatters #VoteThemOut

Tired of chaos? Dump dumb Trump and breathe. #Bye-Don #DumpTheDumb #DumpTrump #EnoughIsEnough #MakeAmericaThinkAgain

Tired of chaos? Dump dumb Trump and breathe. #No-MoreLies #TakeOutTheTrash #TimeForChange #TruthMatters #VoteThemOut

We're not a reality show. #ByeDon #DumpTheDumb #DumpTrump #EnoughIsEnough #MakeAmericaThink-Again

We're not a reality show. #NoMoreLies #TakeOut-TheTrash #TimeForChange #TruthMatters #VoteTh-emOut

CHAPTER 5: 281 ANGRY ANTI-TRUMP SENTENCES

Destroy the chaos — dump Trump before democracy becomes a joke.

Destroy the chaos — dump Trump before he burns down the last bit of trust we have.

Destroy the chaos — dump Trump before he destroys everything we stand for.

Destroy the chaos — dump Trump before he pulls us into more hate and division.

Destroy the chaos — dump Trump before his grift collapses us all.

Destroy the chaos — dump Trump before our country crumbles under his incompetence.

Destroy the chaos — dump Trump before the world laughs at us.

Destroy the chaos — dump Trump before we lose our dignity and rights.

Destroy the chaos — dump Trump before we sink into the abyss of his lies.

Destroy the chaos — dump Trump before we're all dragged into his madness.

Dump the dumb Trump before democracy becomes a joke.

Dump the dumb Trump before he burns down the last bit of trust we have.

Dump the dumb Trump before he destroys everything we stand for.

Dump the dumb Trump before he pulls us into more hate and division.

Dump the dumb Trump before his grift collapses us all.

Dump the dumb Trump before our country crumbles under his incompetence.

Dump the dumb Trump before the world laughs at us.

Dump the dumb Trump before we lose our dignity and rights.

Dump the dumb Trump before we sink into the abyss of his lies.

Dump the dumb Trump before we're all dragged into his madness.

Enough is enough with the bigotry Trump promotes.

Enough is enough with the chaos Trump leaves behind.

Enough is enough with the destruction Trump glorifies.

Enough is enough with the ignorance that Trump represents.

Enough is enough with the lies spewed by Trump.

Enough is enough with Trump's attacks on decency and truth.

Enough is enough with Trump's cult of corruption.

Enough is enough with Trump's endless stream of hate.

Enough is enough with Trump's reckless abuse of power.

Enough is enough with Trump's toxic leadership.

Enough of this nonsense — dump Trump before democracy becomes a joke.

Enough of this nonsense — dump Trump before he burns down the last bit of trust we have.

Enough of this nonsense — dump Trump before he destroys everything we stand for.

Enough of this nonsense — dump Trump before he pulls us into more hate and division.

Enough of this nonsense — dump Trump before his grift collapses us all.

Enough of this nonsense — dump Trump before our country crumbles under his incompetence.

Enough of this nonsense — dump Trump before the world laughs at us.

Enough of this nonsense — dump Trump before we lose our dignity and rights.

Enough of this nonsense — dump Trump before we sink into the abyss of his lies.

Enough of this nonsense — dump Trump before we're all dragged into his madness.

It's time to crush the lies and dump Trump before democracy becomes a joke.

It's time to crush the lies and dump Trump before he burns down the last bit of trust we have.

It's time to crush the lies and dump Trump before he destroys everything we stand for.

It's time to crush the lies and dump Trump before he pulls us into more hate and division.

It's time to crush the lies and dump Trump before his grift collapses us all.

It's time to crush the lies and dump Trump before our country crumbles under his incompetence.

It's time to crush the lies and dump Trump before the world laughs at us.

It's time to crush the lies and dump Trump before we lose our dignity and rights.

It's time to crush the lies and dump Trump before we sink into the abyss of his lies.

It's time to crush the lies and dump Trump before we're all dragged into his madness.

It's time to end the bigotry Trump promotes.

It's time to end the chaos Trump leaves behind.

It's time to end the destruction Trump glorifies.

It's time to end the ignorance that Trump represents.

It's time to end the lies spewed by Trump.

It's time to end Trump's attacks on decency and truth.

It's time to end Trump's cult of corruption.

It's time to end Trump's endless stream of hate.

It's time to end Trump's reckless abuse of power.

It's time to end Trump's toxic leadership.

No more excuses — dump Trump before democracy becomes a joke.

No more excuses — dump Trump before he burns down the last bit of trust we have.

No more excuses — dump Trump before he destroys everything we stand for.

No more excuses — dump Trump before he pulls us into more hate and division.

No more excuses — dump Trump before his grift collapses us all.

No more excuses — dump Trump before our country crumbles under his incompetence.

No more excuses — dump Trump before the world laughs at us.

No more excuses — dump Trump before we lose our dignity and rights.

No more excuses — dump Trump before we sink into the abyss of his lies.

No more excuses — dump Trump before we're all dragged into his madness.

No more the bigotry Trump promotes.

No more the chaos Trump leaves behind.

No more the destruction Trump glorifies.

No more the ignorance that Trump represents.

No more the lies spewed by Trump.

No more Trump's attacks on decency and truth.

No more Trump's cult of corruption.

No more Trump's endless stream of hate.

No more Trump's reckless abuse of power.

No more Trump's toxic leadership.

Stop the madness — dump Trump before democracy becomes a joke.

Stop the madness — dump Trump before he burns down the last bit of trust we have.

Stop the madness — dump Trump before he destroys everything we stand for.

Stop the madness — dump Trump before he pulls us into more hate and division.

Stop the madness — dump Trump before his grift collapses us all.

Stop the madness — dump Trump before our country crumbles under his incompetence.

Stop the madness — dump Trump before the world laughs at us.

Stop the madness — dump Trump before we lose our dignity and rights.

Stop the madness — dump Trump before we sink into the abyss of his lies.

Stop the madness — dump Trump before we're all dragged into his madness.

The lies must end now — dump Trump before democracy becomes a joke.

The lies must end now — dump Trump before he burns down the last bit of trust we have.

The lies must end now — dump Trump before he destroys everything we stand for.

The lies must end now — dump Trump before he pulls us into more hate and division.

The lies must end now — dump Trump before his grift collapses us all.

The lies must end now — dump Trump before our country crumbles under his incompetence.

The lies must end now — dump Trump before the world laughs at us.

The lies must end now — dump Trump before we lose our dignity and rights.

The lies must end now — dump Trump before we sink into the abyss of his lies.

The lies must end now — dump Trump before we're all dragged into his madness.

There's no excuse for the bigotry Trump promotes.

There's no excuse for the chaos Trump leaves behind.

There's no excuse for the destruction Trump glorifies.

There's no excuse for the ignorance that Trump represents.

There's no excuse for the lies spewed by Trump.

There's no excuse for Trump's attacks on decency and truth.

There's no excuse for Trump's cult of corruption.

There's no excuse for Trump's endless stream of hate.

There's no excuse for Trump's reckless abuse of power.

There's no excuse for Trump's toxic leadership.

We cannot stand for before democracy becomes a joke.

We cannot stand for before he burns down the last bit of trust we have.

We cannot stand for before he destroys everything we stand for.

We cannot stand for before he pulls us into more hate and division.

We cannot stand for before his grift collapses us all.

We cannot stand for before our country crumbles under his incompetence.

We cannot stand for before the world laughs at us.

We cannot stand for before we lose our dignity and rights.

We cannot stand for before we sink into the abyss of his lies.

We cannot stand for before we're all dragged into his madness.

We must destroy the bigotry Trump promotes.

We must destroy the chaos Trump leaves behind.

We must destroy the destruction Trump glorifies.

We must destroy the ignorance that Trump represents.

We must destroy the lies spewed by Trump.

We must destroy Trump's attacks on decency and truth.

We must destroy Trump's cult of corruption.

We must destroy Trump's endless stream of hate.

We must destroy Trump's reckless abuse of power.

We must destroy Trump's toxic leadership.

We must rise against the bigotry Trump promotes.

We must rise against the chaos Trump leaves behind.

We must rise against the destruction Trump glorifies.

We must rise against the ignorance that Trump represents.

We must rise against the lies spewed by Trump.

We must rise against Trump's attacks on decency and truth.

We must rise against Trump's cult of corruption.

We must rise against Trump's endless stream of hate.

We must rise against Trump's reckless abuse of power.

We must rise against Trump's toxic leadership.

We reject the bigotry Trump promotes.

We reject the chaos Trump leaves behind.

We reject the destruction Trump glorifies.

We reject the ignorance that Trump represents.

We reject the lies spewed by Trump.

We reject Trump's attacks on decency and truth.

We reject Trump's cult of corruption.

We reject Trump's endless stream of hate.

We reject Trump's reckless abuse of power.

We reject Trump's toxic leadership.

We will not accept the bigotry Trump promotes.

We will not accept the chaos Trump leaves behind.

We will not accept the destruction Trump glorifies.

We will not accept the ignorance that Trump represents.

We will not accept the lies spewed by Trump.

We will not accept Trump's attacks on decency and truth.

We will not accept Trump's cult of corruption.

We will not accept Trump's endless stream of hate.

We will not accept Trump's reckless abuse of power.

We will not accept Trump's toxic leadership.

We're done tolerating the bigotry Trump promotes.

We're done tolerating the chaos Trump leaves behind.

We're done tolerating the destruction Trump glorifies.

We're done tolerating the ignorance that Trump represents.

We're done tolerating the lies spewed by Trump.

We're done tolerating Trump's attacks on decency and truth.

We're done tolerating Trump's cult of corruption.

We're done tolerating Trump's endless stream of hate.

We're done tolerating Trump's reckless abuse of power.

We're done tolerating Trump's toxic leadership.

We've been patient too long — dump Trump before democracy becomes a joke.

We've been patient too long — dump Trump before he burns down the last bit of trust we have.

We've been patient too long — dump Trump before he destroys everything we stand for.

We've been patient too long — dump Trump before he pulls us into more hate and division.

We've been patient too long — dump Trump before his grift collapses us all.

We've been patient too long — dump Trump before our country crumbles under his incompetence.

We've been patient too long — dump Trump before the world laughs at us.

We've been patient too long — dump Trump before we lose our dignity and rights.

We've been patient too long — dump Trump before we sink into the abyss of his lies.

We've been patient too long — dump Trump before we're all dragged into his madness.

We've had enough of the bigotry Trump promotes.

We've had enough of the chaos Trump leaves behind.

We've had enough of the destruction Trump glorifies.

We've had enough of the ignorance that Trump represents.

We've had enough of the lies spewed by Trump.

We've had enough of Trump's attacks on decency and truth.

We've had enough of Trump's cult of corruption.

We've had enough of Trump's endless stream of hate.

We've had enough of Trump's reckless abuse of power.

We've had enough of Trump's toxic leadership.

We've had enough of Trump's toxicity, so dump Trump before democracy becomes a joke.

We've had enough of Trump's toxicity, so dump Trump before he burns down the last bit of trust we have.

We've had enough of Trump's toxicity, so dump Trump before he destroys everything we stand for.

We've had enough of Trump's toxicity, so dump Trump before he pulls us into more hate and division.

We've had enough of Trump's toxicity, so dump Trump before his grift collapses us all.

We've had enough of Trump's toxicity, so dump Trump before our country crumbles under his incompetence.

We've had enough of Trump's toxicity, so dump Trump before the world laughs at us.

We've had enough of Trump's toxicity, so dump Trump before we lose our dignity and rights.

We've had enough of Trump's toxicity, so dump Trump before we sink into the abyss of his lies.

We've had enough of Trump's toxicity, so dump Trump before we're all dragged into his madness.

The lies must end now — dump before we're all dragged into his madness.

No more excuses — dump before his grift collapses us all.

We've had enough of Trump's toxicity, so dump before he destroys everything we stand for.

No more excuses — dump before we sink into the abyss of his lies.

Destroy the chaos — dump before we lose our dignity and rights.

We've been patient too long — dump before our country crumbles under his incompetence.

We've been patient too long — dump before he burns down the last bit of trust we have.

The lies must end now — dump before democracy becomes a joke.

We've had enough of Trump's toxicity, so dump before our country crumbles under his incompetence.

Destroy the chaos — dump before our country crumbles under his incompetence.

We've had enough of Trump's toxicity, so dump before we sink into the abyss of his lies.

No more excuses — dump before the world laughs at us.

Enough of this nonsense — dump before the world laughs at us.

The lies must end now — dump before we lose our dignity and rights.

Stop the madness — dump before we're all dragged into his madness.

The lies must end now — dump before the world laughs at us.

Stop the madness — dump before he burns down the last bit of trust we have.

The lies must end now — dump before he destroys everything we stand for.

It's time to crush the lies and dump before our country crumbles under his incompetence.

Destroy the chaos — dump before he burns down the last bit of trust we have.

Stop the madness — dump before the world laughs at us.

It's time to crush the lies and dump before he destroys everything we stand for.

Enough of this nonsense — dump before democracy becomes a joke.

Enough of this nonsense — dump before he destroys everything we stand for.

No more excuses — dump before our country crumbles under his incompetence.

Enough of this nonsense — dump before his grift collapses us all.

Enough of this nonsense — dump before he burns down the last bit of trust we have.

Destroy the chaos — dump before the world laughs at us.

Enough of this nonsense — dump before our country crumbles under his incompetence.

We've had enough of Trump's toxicity, so dump before his grift collapses us all.

It's time to crush the lies and dump before he pulls us into more hate and division.

Destroy the chaos — dump before democracy becomes a joke.

It's time to crush the lies and dump before we're all dragged into his madness.

We've had enough of Trump's toxicity, so dump before he burns down the last bit of trust we have.

We've been patient too long — dump before we're all dragged into his madness.

Destroy the chaos — dump before he destroys everything we stand for.

We've been patient too long — dump before democracy becomes a joke.

The lies must end now — dump before our country crumbles under his incompetence.

We've been patient too long — dump before we lose our dignity and rights.

Stop the madness — dump before he destroys everything we stand for.

Stop the madness — dump before democracy becomes a joke.

We've been patient too long — dump before he destroys everything we stand for.

No more excuses — dump before we lose our dignity and rights.

The lies must end now — dump before we sink into the abyss of his lies.

It's time to crush the lies and dump before we lose our dignity and rights.

Destroy the chaos — dump before he pulls us into more hate and division.

Enough of this nonsense — dump before he pulls us into more hate and division.

It's time to crush the lies and dump before democracy becomes a joke.

We've had enough of Trump's toxicity, so dump before the world laughs at us.

We've had enough of Trump's toxicity, so dump before democracy becomes a joke.

No more excuses — dump before he pulls us into more hate and division.

No more excuses — dump before he destroys everything we stand for.

Enough of this nonsense — dump before we sink into the abyss of his lies.

The lies must end now — dump before he pulls us into more hate and division.

No more excuses — dump before democracy becomes a joke.

Enough of this nonsense — dump before we're all dragged into his madness.

Stop the madness — dump before his grift collapses us all.

Stop the madness — dump before we lose our dignity and rights.

We've been patient too long — dump before we sink into the abyss of his lies.

No more excuses — dump before he burns down the last bit of trust we have.

Enough of this nonsense — dump before we lose our dignity and rights.

We've had enough of Trump's toxicity, so dump before we lose our dignity and rights.

Destroy the chaos — dump before his grift collapses us all.

We've been patient too long — dump before he pulls us into more hate and division.

The lies must end now — dump before he burns down the last bit of trust we have.

We've been patient too long — dump before the world laughs at us.

It's time to crush the lies and dump before his grift collapses us all.

No more excuses — dump before we're all dragged into his madness.

Stop the madness — dump before our country crumbles under his incompetence.

We've had enough of Trump's toxicity, so dump before we're all dragged into his madness.

The lies must end now — dump before his grift collapses us all.

We've been patient too long — dump before his grift collapses us all.

Destroy the chaos — dump before we're all dragged into his madness.

Stop the madness — dump before he pulls us into more hate and division.

It's time to crush the lies and dump before he burns down the last bit of trust we have.

Destroy the chaos — dump before we sink into the abyss of his lies.

We've had enough of Trump's toxicity, so dump before he pulls us into more hate and division.

It's time to crush the lies and dump before the world laughs at us.

It's time to crush the lies and dump before we sink into the abyss of his lies.

Stop the madness — dump before we sink into the abyss of his lies.

Yeet that man like a fax machine in a TikTok office.

Toss Trump out like the last slice of gas station sushi.

Get rid of Trump like your ex's mixtape.

Yeet that man like a dial-up modem at a LAN party.

Drop Trump like a glitter bomb at a funeral.

Banish Trump like a cursed group chat.

Banish Trump like a glitter bomb at a funeral.

Drop Trump like a cursed group chat.

Boot Trump like a dial-up modem at a LAN party.

Yeet that man like an MLM invite from your aunt.

Get rid of Trump like a cursed group chat.

Boot Trump like a wet sock in cold weather.

Dump dumb Trump like a fax machine in a TikTok office.

Dump dumb Trump like an MLM invite from your aunt.

Yeet that man like the last slice of gas station sushi.

Drop Trump like a dial-up modem at a LAN party.

Ditch dumb Trump like an MLM invite from your aunt.

Drop Trump like an MLM invite from your aunt.

Boot Trump like a cursed group chat.

Toss Trump out like a wet sock in cold weather.

Dump dumb Trump like the last slice of gas station sushi.

Get rid of Trump like expired milk on a summer day.

Get rid of Trump like the last slice of gas station sushi.

Ditch dumb Trump like Windows 95 in 2025.

Banish Trump like an MLM invite from your aunt.

Ditch dumb Trump like a dial-up modem at a LAN party.

Toss Trump out like Windows 95 in 2025.

Ditch dumb Trump like a fax machine in a TikTok office.

Ditch dumb Trump like expired milk on a summer day.
Eject Trump faster than a glitter bomb at a funeral.
Boot Trump like Windows 95 in 2025.
Send Trump packing like your ex's mixtape.
Boot Trump like your ex's mixtape.
Eject Trump faster than the last slice of gas station sushi.
Banish Trump like a fax machine in a TikTok office.
Yeet that man like a wet sock in cold weather.
Eject Trump faster than expired milk on a summer day.
Banish Trump like a dial-up modem at a LAN party.
Get rid of Trump like Windows 95 in 2025.
Banish Trump like Windows 95 in 2025.
Ditch dumb Trump like your ex's mixtape.
Yeet that man like a glitter bomb at a funeral.
Dump dumb Trump like Windows 95 in 2025.
Yeet that man like a cursed group chat.
Eject Trump faster than a cursed group chat.
Send Trump packing like the last slice of gas station sushi.
Get rid of Trump like a glitter bomb at a funeral.
Toss Trump out like your ex's mixtape.
Get rid of Trump like a fax machine in a TikTok office.
Boot Trump like an MLM invite from your aunt.
Send Trump packing like a wet sock in cold weather.
Dump dumb Trump like your ex's mixtape.
Boot Trump like a fax machine in a TikTok office.
Toss Trump out like a dial-up modem at a LAN party.
Drop Trump like the last slice of gas station sushi.
Send Trump packing like Windows 95 in 2025.
Send Trump packing like a dial-up modem at a LAN party.
Send Trump packing like expired milk on a summer day.
Boot Trump like expired milk on a summer day.
Toss Trump out like a cursed group chat.
Dump dumb Trump like a glitter bomb at a funeral.
Toss Trump out like a fax machine in a TikTok office.

Yeet that man like expired milk on a summer day.

Drop Trump like Windows 95 in 2025.

Eject Trump faster than a dial-up modem at a LAN party.

Toss Trump out like a glitter bomb at a funeral.

Drop Trump like your ex's mixtape.

Send Trump packing like a fax machine in a TikTok office.

Yeet that man like your ex's mixtape.

Ditch dumb Trump like a wet sock in cold weather.

Dump dumb Trump like a wet sock in cold weather.

Eject Trump faster than your ex's mixtape.

Drop Trump like a fax machine in a TikTok office.

Banish Trump like a wet sock in cold weather.

Eject Trump faster than an MLM invite from your aunt.

Banish Trump like your ex's mixtape.

Toss Trump out like expired milk on a summer day.

Ditch dumb Trump like a glitter bomb at a funeral.

Yeet that man like Windows 95 in 2025.

Drop Trump like a wet sock in cold weather.

Toss Trump out like an MLM invite from your aunt.

Dump dumb Trump like a cursed group chat.

Send Trump packing like a cursed group chat.

Get rid of Trump like a wet sock in cold weather.

Dump dumb Trump like expired milk on a summer day.

Eject Trump faster than a fax machine in a TikTok office.

Boot Trump like the last slice of gas station sushi.

Ditch dumb Trump like the last slice of gas station sushi.

Drop Trump like expired milk on a summer day.

Send Trump packing like an MLM invite from your aunt.

Banish Trump like expired milk on a summer day.

Eject Trump faster than Windows 95 in 2025.

Send Trump packing like a glitter bomb at a funeral.

Boot Trump like a glitter bomb at a funeral.

Eject Trump faster than a wet sock in cold weather.

Banish Trump like the last slice of gas station sushi.

Get rid of Trump like an MLM invite from your aunt.
Get rid of Trump like a dial-up modem at a LAN party.
Ditch dumb Trump like a cursed group chat.
Dump dumb Trump like a dial-up modem at a LAN party.

Act now—dump dumb Trump and uphold the constitution

Stand strong — dump dumb Trump for good

Keep calm and dump dumb Trump for good

Unite to dump dumb Trump and choose reason

Unite to dump dumb Trump before it's too late

Act now—dump dumb Trump and build real leadership

Dump the dumb Trump and reclaim our nation

DUMP DUMB TRUMP NOW!

Take action: dump dumb Trump and reclaim our nation

Unite to dump dumb Trump and build real leadership

No mercy — dump dumb Trump and rebuild trust

Freedom means dump dumb Trump and rebuild trust

Dump Dumb Trump and reclaim our nation

Together we dump dumb Trump and protect the truth

Keep calm and dump dumb Trump and protect the truth

Democracy demands we dump dumb Trump and stand for justice

Dump the dumb Trump and save our future

Act now—dump dumb Trump for good

Hands up for dumping dumb Trump and protect the truth

Take action: dump dumb Trump and reject corruption

Together we dump dumb Trump and rebuild trust

Time to dump dumb Trump and protect the truth

No mercy — dump dumb Trump before it's too late

Now is the time: dump dumb Trump and restore democracy

Act now—dump dumb Trump NOW!

Now is the time: dump dumb Trump and end the lies

Our future: dump dumb Trump and reject hate

No mercy — dump dumb Trump and end the lies

Our future: dump dumb Trump and protect the truth

Time to dump dumb Trump and reject corruption

March on and dump dumb Trump and rebuild trust

We the people say: dump dumb Trump and reject corruption

Dump the dumb Trump and uphold the constitution

No mercy — dump dumb Trump and reject chaos

Dump Dumb Trump and reject hate

No mercy — dump dumb Trump and save our future

Take action: dump dumb Trump NOW!

Dump Dumb Trump and end the lies

DUMP DUMB TRUMP and reject corruption

Keep calm and dump dumb Trump and choose reason

Dump the dumb Trump NOW!

DUMP DUMB TRUMP and save our future

March on and dump dumb Trump and reject corruption

Unite to dump dumb Trump and reject corruption

Together we dump dumb Trump and build real leadership

Together we dump dumb Trump and defend our rights

Time to dump dumb Trump and reject chaos

Democracy demands we dump dumb Trump and embrace facts

Unite to dump dumb Trump and restore democracy

No mercy — dump dumb Trump and uphold the constitution

Freedom means dump dumb Trump and defend our rights

We the people say: dump dumb Trump and defend our rights

Stand strong — dump dumb Trump and end the lies

March on and dump dumb Trump and defend our rights

Dump the dumb Trump and reject corruption

Stand strong — dump dumb Trump and reclaim our nation

Time to dump dumb Trump and choose reason

We the people say: dump dumb Trump and reject chaos

Democracy demands we dump dumb Trump and honor the rule of law

Justice calls: dump dumb Trump and reject hate

Keep calm and dump dumb Trump and end the lies

We the people say: dump dumb Trump before it's too late

We the people say: dump dumb Trump and embrace facts

Take action: dump dumb Trump and build real leadership

Stand strong — dump dumb Trump and stand for justice

Justice calls: dump dumb Trump and defend our rights

Time to dump dumb Trump and reject hate

Unite to dump dumb Trump and save our future

Hands up for dumping dumb Trump and unite our people

Now is the time: dump dumb Trump before it's too late

No mercy — dump dumb Trump and reclaim our nation

March on and dump dumb Trump and choose reason

Now is the time: dump dumb Trump and defend our rights

Dump the dumb Trump and embrace facts

Democracy demands we dump dumb Trump and protect the truth

Hands up for dumping dumb Trump and honor the rule of law

Act now—dump dumb Trump and reject hate

DUMP DUMB TRUMP and embrace facts

No mercy — dump dumb Trump for good

Keep calm and dump dumb Trump and honor the rule of law

DUMP DUMB TRUMP and restore democracy

Keep calm and dump dumb Trump before it's too late

DUMP DUMB TRUMP and unite our people

Freedom means dump dumb Trump for good

March on and dump dumb Trump for good

Together we dump dumb Trump NOW!

Take action: dump dumb Trump and protect the truth

Hands up for dumping dumb Trump and reject hate

Hands up for dumping dumb Trump before it's too late

Rise up — dump dumb Trump and unite our people

Now is the time: dump dumb Trump and build real leadership

Justice calls: dump dumb Trump and rebuild trust

Dump Dumb Trump and rebuild trust

March on and dump dumb Trump and honor the rule of
law

Act now—dump dumb Trump and unite our people

Together we dump dumb Trump and reject corruption

Dump the dumb Trump and build real leadership

March on and dump dumb Trump before it's too late

Rise up — dump dumb Trump and reject chaos

Justice calls: dump dumb Trump and reject chaos

Time to dump dumb Trump and stand for justice

Now is the time: dump dumb Trump for good

DUMP DUMB TRUMP and defend our rights

We the people say: dump dumb Trump for good

Hands up for dumping dumb Trump for good

Democracy demands we dump dumb Trump and defend
our rights

Stand strong — dump dumb Trump and unite our people

Time to dump dumb Trump and rebuild trust

Dump the dumb Trump and restore democracy

Our future: dump dumb Trump and defend our rights

Dump the dumb Trump and reject chaos

Together we dump dumb Trump and save our future

Rise up — dump dumb Trump and rebuild trust

Unite to dump dumb Trump and honor the rule of law

Justice calls: dump dumb Trump for good

We the people say: dump dumb Trump and unite our people

Act now—dump dumb Trump and reclaim our nation
Keep calm and dump dumb Trump and stand for justice
Democracy demands we dump dumb Trump and end the lies
Hands up for dumping dumb Trump and save our future
Keep calm and dump dumb Trump and reject hate
March on and dump dumb Trump and restore democracy
Together we dump dumb Trump and restore democracy
Keep calm and dump dumb Trump and embrace facts
Take action: dump dumb Trump and choose reason
Hands up for dumping dumb Trump NOW!
No mercy — dump dumb Trump and choose reason
Take action: dump dumb Trump and defend our rights
Act now—dump dumb Trump and choose reason
Together we dump dumb Trump and stand for justice
Stand strong — dump dumb Trump and save our future
Freedom means dump dumb Trump and build real leadership
March on and dump dumb Trump and uphold the constitution
No mercy — dump dumb Trump and protect the truth
No mercy — dump dumb Trump and honor the rule of law
Justice calls: dump dumb Trump and reject corruption
Dump Dumb Trump and protect the truth
Stand strong — dump dumb Trump and defend our rights
Dump Dumb Trump and reject chaos
Now is the time: dump dumb Trump and reject chaos
Take action: dump dumb Trump and unite our people
Together we dump dumb Trump and unite our people
Time to dump dumb Trump and defend our rights
Democracy demands we dump dumb Trump before it's too late
Keep calm and dump dumb Trump and build real leadership

DUMP DUMB TRUMP and honor the rule of law

We the people say: dump dumb Trump and protect the truth

Justice calls: dump dumb Trump and reclaim our nation

Keep calm and dump dumb Trump and reclaim our nation

Our future: dump dumb Trump and honor the rule of law

Freedom means dump dumb Trump and restore democracy

Democracy demands we dump dumb Trump and reject chaos

Act now—dump dumb Trump and end the lies

Our future: dump dumb Trump before it's too late

DUMP DUMB TRUMP before it's too late

Our future: dump dumb Trump and stand for justice

Take action: dump dumb Trump and end the lies

Hands up for dumping dumb Trump and restore democracy

Our future: dump dumb Trump and embrace facts

Keep calm and dump dumb Trump and save our future

Act now—dump dumb Trump and embrace facts

Freedom means dump dumb Trump NOW!

Freedom means dump dumb Trump and protect the truth

Stand strong — dump dumb Trump before it's too late

Unite to dump dumb Trump and rebuild trust

Freedom means dump dumb Trump and honor the rule of law

Time to dump dumb Trump and save our future

Now is the time: dump dumb Trump and protect the truth

Democracy demands we dump dumb Trump and uphold the constitution

No mercy — dump dumb Trump and embrace facts

Freedom means dump dumb Trump and reject hate

Unite to dump dumb Trump and embrace facts

Time to dump dumb Trump and honor the rule of law

March on and dump dumb Trump NOW!

Now is the time: dump dumb Trump NOW!

Dump the dumb Trump and rebuild trust

Together we dump dumb Trump and honor the rule of law

Keep calm and dump dumb Trump and uphold the constitution

Act now — dump dumb Trump and reject corruption

Keep calm and dump dumb Trump and defend our rights

Rise up — dump dumb Trump NOW!

Act now — dump dumb Trump and restore democracy

Rise up — dump dumb Trump and end the lies

Time to dump dumb Trump NOW!

March on and dump dumb Trump and reject chaos

Now is the time: dump dumb Trump and honor the rule of law

Justice calls: dump dumb Trump and choose reason

Our future: dump dumb Trump and reject corruption

Justice calls: dump dumb Trump and embrace facts

Hands up for dumping dumb Trump and build real leadership

No mercy — dump dumb Trump and reject hate

Together we dump dumb Trump and end the lies

Dump the dumb Trump and end the lies

Take action: dump dumb Trump and embrace facts

Now is the time: dump dumb Trump and embrace facts

Take action: dump dumb Trump and stand for justice

We the people say: dump dumb Trump and reject hate

Take action: dump dumb Trump and reject chaos

Our future: dump dumb Trump NOW!

Now is the time: dump dumb Trump and unite our people

Rise up — dump dumb Trump for good

Our future: dump dumb Trump and end the lies

Dump Dumb Trump and build real leadership

Democracy demands we dump dumb Trump and reclaim our nation

Hands up for dumping dumb Trump and reclaim our nation

Dump the dumb Trump and reject hate

No mercy — dump dumb Trump and build real leadership

Together we dump dumb Trump before it's too late

Justice calls: dump dumb Trump and end the lies

We the people say: dump dumb Trump NOW!

March on and dump dumb Trump and reject hate

Rise up — dump dumb Trump and defend our rights

Dump the dumb Trump for good

Dump Dumb Trump and choose reason

Now is the time: dump dumb Trump and reject corruption

March on and dump dumb Trump and reclaim our nation

Stand strong — dump dumb Trump and uphold the constitution

Justice calls: dump dumb Trump and unite our people

Together we dump dumb Trump and choose reason

Take action: dump dumb Trump and uphold the constitution

Stand strong — dump dumb Trump and build real leadership

No mercy — dump dumb Trump and restore democracy

Freedom means dump dumb Trump and unite our people

Time to dump dumb Trump and build real leadership

Rise up — dump dumb Trump and reject corruption

Together we dump dumb Trump and embrace facts

Time to dump dumb Trump and end the lies

We the people say: dump dumb Trump and stand for justice

Unite to dump dumb Trump and reclaim our nation

Take action: dump dumb Trump and restore democracy

March on and dump dumb Trump and save our future

51

Our future: dump dumb Trump and uphold the constitution

Unite to dump dumb Trump and defend our rights

Freedom means dump dumb Trump and save our future

Democracy demands we dump dumb Trump and rebuild trust

Unite to dump dumb Trump and protect the truth

Our future: dump dumb Trump and rebuild trust

Take action: dump dumb Trump for good

DUMP DUMB TRUMP and stand for justice

Justice calls: dump dumb Trump and stand for justice

Act now—dump dumb Trump and defend our rights

Democracy demands we dump dumb Trump and reject hate

Take action: dump dumb Trump and save our future

Dump Dumb Trump and uphold the constitution

Unite to dump dumb Trump and reject hate

March on and dump dumb Trump and unite our people

Act now—dump dumb Trump and stand for justice

Hands up for dumping dumb Trump and uphold the constitution

Act now—dump dumb Trump and rebuild trust

Dump Dumb Trump for good

Rise up — dump dumb Trump and reclaim our nation

Now is the time: dump dumb Trump and stand for justice

Together we dump dumb Trump and uphold the constitution

Time to dump dumb Trump for good

Democracy demands we dump dumb Trump for good

Keep calm and dump dumb Trump and restore democracy

We the people say: dump dumb Trump and choose reason

Unite to dump dumb Trump and stand for justice

Justice calls: dump dumb Trump and save our future

Dump the dumb Trump and choose reason

March on and dump dumb Trump and build real leadership

Freedom means dump dumb Trump and end the lies

Freedom means dump dumb Trump and reject corruption

Justice calls: dump dumb Trump before it's too late

Our future: dump dumb Trump and reject chaos

Justice calls: dump dumb Trump and build real leadership

Our future: dump dumb Trump and choose reason

We the people say: dump dumb Trump and save our future

Freedom means dump dumb Trump and stand for justice

Rise up — dump dumb Trump and honor the rule of law

Hands up for dumping dumb Trump and stand for justice

Democracy demands we dump dumb Trump and unite our people

Rise up — dump dumb Trump and uphold the constitution

Hands up for dumping dumb Trump and reject chaos

We the people say: dump dumb Trump and restore democracy

Rise up — dump dumb Trump and build real leadership

Act now—dump dumb Trump before it's too late

Stand strong — dump dumb Trump and reject chaos

Time to dump dumb Trump and restore democracy

Justice calls: dump dumb Trump and restore democracy

Hands up for dumping dumb Trump and reject corruption

Democracy demands we dump dumb Trump and build real leadership

Democracy demands we dump dumb Trump and choose reason

Freedom means dump dumb Trump and reject chaos

Now is the time: dump dumb Trump and choose reason

Our future: dump dumb Trump for good

Unite to dump dumb Trump and unite our people

Stand strong — dump dumb Trump and reject hate

Keep calm and dump dumb Trump and reject corruption
March on and dump dumb Trump and end the lies
Our future: dump dumb Trump and unite our people
Keep calm and dump dumb Trump NOW!
Rise up — dump dumb Trump and restore democracy
Together we dump dumb Trump for good
Democracy demands we dump dumb Trump and reject corruption
We the people say: dump dumb Trump and reclaim our nation
Dump the dumb Trump and defend our rights
Rise up — dump dumb Trump and reject hate
Democracy demands we dump dumb Trump and restore democracy
Our future: dump dumb Trump and save our future
No mercy — dump dumb Trump NOW!
Unite to dump dumb Trump and end the lies
Together we dump dumb Trump and reject chaos
Democracy demands we dump dumb Trump and save our future
Freedom means dump dumb Trump and choose reason
No mercy — dump dumb Trump and unite our people
Justice calls: dump dumb Trump and protect the truth
Our future: dump dumb Trump and reclaim our nation
Hands up for dumping dumb Trump and defend our rights
Unite to dump dumb Trump NOW!
Act now—dump dumb Trump and protect the truth
Rise up — dump dumb Trump and stand for justice
Hands up for dumping dumb Trump and end the lies
Time to dump dumb Trump and unite our people
Take action: dump dumb Trump and honor the rule of law
Stand strong — dump dumb Trump and reject corruption
Stand strong — dump dumb Trump and rebuild trust
March on and dump dumb Trump and embrace facts

Rise up — dump dumb Trump and protect the truth

Dump the dumb Trump and protect the truth

Dump the dumb Trump and stand for justice

Stand strong — dump dumb Trump and protect the truth

We the people say: dump dumb Trump and uphold the constitution

March on and dump dumb Trump and protect the truth

Now is the time: dump dumb Trump and reclaim our nation

Take action: dump dumb Trump before it's too late

Now is the time: dump dumb Trump and save our future

Dump the dumb Trump before it's too late

Our future: dump dumb Trump and build real leadership

Time to dump dumb Trump and uphold the constitution

No mercy — dump dumb Trump and reject corruption

Time to dump dumb Trump and reclaim our nation

Act now — dump dumb Trump and reject chaos

Rise up — dump dumb Trump and choose reason

Justice calls: dump dumb Trump NOW!

We the people say: dump dumb Trump and end the lies

Hands up for dumping dumb Trump and choose reason

Rise up — dump dumb Trump and embrace facts

Keep calm and dump dumb Trump and reject chaos

Dump the dumb Trump and unite our people

Now is the time: dump dumb Trump and rebuild trust

Stand strong — dump dumb Trump and honor the rule of law

Stand strong — dump dumb Trump and embrace facts

Unite to dump dumb Trump for good

We the people say: dump dumb Trump and build real leadership

Dump the dumb Trump and honor the rule of law

Keep calm and dump dumb Trump and rebuild trust

Stand strong — dump dumb Trump and restore democracy

Justice calls: dump dumb Trump and honor the rule of law

Act now—dump dumb Trump and honor the rule of law

Freedom means dump dumb Trump and reclaim our nation

Now is the time: dump dumb Trump and uphold the constitution

Time to dump dumb Trump before it's too late

March on and dump dumb Trump and stand for justice

We the people say: dump dumb Trump and rebuild trust

Act now—dump dumb Trump and save our future

Democracy demands we dump dumb Trump NOW!

No mercy — dump dumb Trump and stand for justice

Take action: dump dumb Trump and reject hate

Unite to dump dumb Trump and uphold the constitution

Take action: dump dumb Trump and rebuild trust

Hands up for dumping dumb Trump and rebuild trust

We the people say: dump dumb Trump and honor the rule of law

Time to dump dumb Trump and embrace facts

Stand strong — dump dumb Trump NOW!

Hands up for dumping dumb Trump and embrace facts

Together we dump dumb Trump and reclaim our nation

Stand strong — dump dumb Trump and choose reason

Together we dump dumb Trump and reject hate

Justice calls: dump dumb Trump and uphold the constitution

Our future: dump dumb Trump and restore democracy

Rise up — dump dumb Trump and save our future

Freedom means dump dumb Trump before it's too late

No mercy — dump dumb Trump and defend our rights

Rise up — dump dumb Trump before it's too late

Freedom means dump dumb Trump and embrace facts

Keep calm and dump dumb Trump and unite our people

Freedom means dump dumb Trump and uphold the constitution

Now is the time: dump dumb Trump and reject hate
Unite to dump dumb Trump and reject chaos.

It's time to remove Trump's attacks on democracy.

Voters should denounce a presidency built on lies and division.

It's time to disqualify Trump's ongoing misinformation.

To protect our values, we must stand against the dangerous leadership of Trump.

We must reject a culture of corruption led by Trump.

Voters should disqualify the erosion of truth under Trump.

We must disqualify a culture of corruption led by Trump.

In defense of democracy, we should stand against a culture of corruption led by Trump.

For the future, we must disempower Trump's attacks on democracy.

We must oppose Trump's harmful influence on the nation.

History will remember those who abandon a presidency built on lies and division.

Voters should vote out Trump's ongoing misinformation.

It's time to stand against Trump's ongoing misinformation.

History will remember those who vote out the erosion of truth under Trump.

Americans deserve to remove the damage done under Trump's watch.

In defense of democracy, we should reject Trump's harmful influence on the nation.

It's time to disqualify Trump's attacks on democracy.

To protect our values, we must vote out the erosion of truth under Trump.

Voters should reject the dangerous leadership of Trump.

Voters should abandon Trump's ongoing misinformation.

Voters should reject Trump's harmful influence on the nation.

Americans deserve to turn away from the chaos and incompetence of Trump.

The nation needs to vote out the chaos and incompetence of Trump.

To protect our values, we must oppose Trump's abuse of power.

Voters should oppose the damage done under Trump's watch.

The only responsible action is to abandon Trump's abuse of power.

Voters should vote out the dangerous leadership of Trump.

Voters should remove the chaos and incompetence of Trump.

The only responsible action is to abandon Trump's ongoing misinformation.

Voters should disempower the chaos and incompetence of Trump.

Voters should turn away from Trump's harmful influence on the nation.

For the future, we must oppose Trump's attacks on democracy.

The nation needs to denounce Trump's abuse of power.

In defense of democracy, we should abandon the erosion of truth under Trump.

The only responsible action is to disempower Trump's harmful influence on the nation.

History will remember those who denounce a presidency built on lies and division.

In defense of democracy, we should turn away from Trump's ongoing misinformation.

We must reject a presidency built on lies and division.

The nation needs to stand against the erosion of truth under Trump.

It's time to stand against Trump's harmful influence on the nation.

To protect our values, we must turn away from Trump's abuse of power.

Americans deserve to disqualify the dangerous leadership of Trump.

History will remember those who reject Trump's attacks on democracy.

The only responsible action is to oppose the damage done under Trump's watch.

We must abandon Trump's abuse of power.

The nation needs to disqualify Trump's ongoing misinformation.

Americans deserve to disqualify the erosion of truth under Trump.

Voters should oppose the chaos and incompetence of Trump.

The nation needs to disqualify Trump's abuse of power.

We must disempower the chaos and incompetence of Trump.

For the future, we must remove Trump's ongoing misinformation.

History will remember those who abandon a culture of corruption led by Trump.

We must denounce the erosion of truth under Trump.

It's time to reject the damage done under Trump's watch.

It's time to disqualify a presidency built on lies and division.

The nation needs to turn away from Trump's abuse of power.

The nation needs to abandon Trump's abuse of power.

To protect our values, we must stand against a culture of corruption led by Trump.

In defense of democracy, we should denounce Trump's attacks on democracy.

The only responsible action is to vote out the damage done under Trump's watch.

Voters should denounce Trump's ongoing misinformation.

History will remember those who remove the erosion of truth under Trump.

In defense of democracy, we should denounce the erosion of truth under Trump.

Voters should remove Trump's ongoing misinformation.

We must denounce Trump's ongoing misinformation.

We must vote out Trump's ongoing misinformation.

For the future, we must denounce Trump's abuse of power.

The nation needs to disempower the erosion of truth under Trump.

For the future, we must denounce the damage done under Trump's watch.

The only responsible action is to denounce Trump's ongoing misinformation.

It's time to stand against the chaos and incompetence of Trump.

The only responsible action is to stand against the damage done under Trump's watch.

We must reject the dangerous leadership of Trump.

The only responsible action is to vote out Trump's ongoing misinformation.

Voters should denounce a culture of corruption led by Trump.

In defense of democracy, we should turn away from a presidency built on lies and division.

The only responsible action is to oppose Trump's attacks on democracy.

For the future, we must denounce Trump's ongoing misinformation.

For the future, we must disqualify Trump's ongoing misinformation.

We must disqualify the dangerous leadership of Trump.

It's time to denounce a presidency built on lies and division.

The only responsible action is to turn away from the damage done under Trump's watch.

Voters should stand against the dangerous leadership of Trump.

The nation needs to stand against the dangerous leadership of Trump.

The only responsible action is to abandon the damage done under Trump's watch.

Americans deserve to stand against Trump's abuse of power.

For the future, we must oppose a culture of corruption led by Trump.

Americans deserve to denounce the dangerous leadership of Trump.

To protect our values, we must disqualify the dangerous leadership of Trump.

History will remember those who remove the dangerous leadership of Trump.

In defense of democracy, we should oppose the dangerous leadership of Trump.

In defense of democracy, we should reject a presidency built on lies and division.

It's time to disempower Trump's ongoing misinformation.

Voters should stand against Trump's ongoing misinformation.

To protect our values, we must denounce the erosion of truth under Trump.

To protect our values, we must remove the erosion of truth under Trump.

It's time to stand against the erosion of truth under Trump.

To protect our values, we must disqualify the chaos and incompetence of Trump.

Americans deserve to denounce the chaos and incompetence of Trump.

Voters should abandon Trump's harmful influence on the nation.

The nation needs to abandon the damage done under Trump's watch.

History will remember those who reject the dangerous leadership of Trump.

For the future, we must disempower the erosion of truth under Trump.

It's time to reject Trump's abuse of power.

Voters should disqualify Trump's attacks on democracy.

The nation needs to vote out Trump's ongoing misinformation.

Voters should vote out Trump's attacks on democracy.

Americans deserve to disempower Trump's abuse of power.

We must disqualify Trump's attacks on democracy.

It's time to oppose Trump's attacks on democracy.

The nation needs to abandon Trump's attacks on democracy.

To protect our values, we must denounce the chaos and incompetence of Trump.

Voters should abandon Trump's abuse of power.

For the future, we must abandon the dangerous leadership of Trump.

It's time to stand against Trump's attacks on democracy.

We must remove the chaos and incompetence of Trump.

The nation needs to abandon a presidency built on lies and division.

For the future, we must disqualify Trump's harmful influence on the nation.

In defense of democracy, we should remove Trump's ongoing misinformation.

It's time to oppose Trump's abuse of power.

We must vote out the erosion of truth under Trump.

In defense of democracy, we should oppose Trump's harmful influence on the nation.

The nation needs to remove Trump's attacks on democracy.

History will remember those who remove the chaos and incompetence of Trump.

History will remember those who disqualify Trump's harmful influence on the nation.

To protect our values, we must oppose a culture of corruption led by Trump.

The nation needs to oppose Trump's harmful influence on the nation.

We must oppose the chaos and incompetence of Trump.

The only responsible action is to denounce Trump's attacks on democracy.

The nation needs to reject Trump's harmful influence on the nation.

We must turn away from a culture of corruption led by Trump.

Voters should turn away from the chaos and incompetence of Trump.

Americans deserve to denounce a culture of corruption led by Trump.

We must denounce Trump's harmful influence on the nation.

History will remember those who abandon Trump's ongoing misinformation.

Americans deserve to vote out Trump's abuse of power.

The only responsible action is to disqualify the chaos and incompetence of Trump.

We must reject Trump's attacks on democracy.

The nation needs to disempower Trump's attacks on democracy.

We must reject the erosion of truth under Trump.

The only responsible action is to vote out the chaos and incompetence of Trump.

The only responsible action is to disempower Trump's abuse of power.

Voters should abandon the dangerous leadership of Trump.

The only responsible action is to remove Trump's abuse of power.

In defense of democracy, we should denounce the chaos and incompetence of Trump.

The only responsible action is to reject the chaos and incompetence of Trump.

To protect our values, we must vote out Trump's ongoing misinformation.

Americans deserve to disqualify Trump's attacks on democracy.

The only responsible action is to vote out Trump's harmful influence on the nation.

Americans deserve to disqualify a presidency built on lies and division.

Voters should stand against Trump's harmful influence on the nation.

We must abandon Trump's attacks on democracy.

Voters should stand against the erosion of truth under Trump.

To protect our values, we must vote out the damage done under Trump's watch.

For the future, we must turn away from a culture of corruption led by Trump.

It's time to abandon Trump's abuse of power.

Voters should abandon a culture of corruption led by Trump.

Voters should oppose the dangerous leadership of Trump.

We must denounce the damage done under Trump's watch.

To protect our values, we must reject the damage done under Trump's watch.

The only responsible action is to disempower a culture of corruption led by Trump.

The only responsible action is to turn away from Trump's harmful influence on the nation.

It's time to stand against a culture of corruption led by Trump.

The nation needs to disqualify the damage done under Trump's watch.

It's time to turn away from a presidency built on lies and division.

For the future, we must disqualify Trump's abuse of power.

To protect our values, we must disqualify Trump's harmful influence on the nation.

For the future, we must turn away from Trump's attacks on democracy.

For the future, we must denounce Trump's attacks on democracy.

For the future, we must reject Trump's attacks on democracy.

Voters should abandon the chaos and incompetence of Trump.

History will remember those who disqualify Trump's ongoing misinformation.

The nation needs to oppose a culture of corruption led by Trump.

The only responsible action is to oppose a culture of corruption led by Trump.

History will remember those who disqualify the damage done under Trump's watch.

The only responsible action is to remove a culture of corruption led by Trump.

The only responsible action is to stand against the erosion of truth under Trump.

We must disempower Trump's harmful influence on the nation.

For the future, we must remove the chaos and incompetence of Trump.

Americans deserve to stand against Trump's harmful influence on the nation.

In defense of democracy, we should disqualify the erosion of truth under Trump.

Voters should turn away from a culture of corruption led by Trump.

Americans deserve to stand against the damage done under Trump's watch.

We must stand against the chaos and incompetence of Trump.

The nation needs to disempower Trump's abuse of power.

We must stand against the erosion of truth under Trump.

To protect our values, we must remove Trump's ongoing misinformation.

The only responsible action is to vote out a culture of corruption led by Trump.

For the future, we must vote out the chaos and incompetence of Trump.

The only responsible action is to abandon Trump's harmful influence on the nation.

Americans deserve to reject the damage done under Trump's watch.

History will remember those who denounce Trump's ongoing misinformation.

We must remove a culture of corruption led by Trump.

Voters should remove the erosion of truth under Trump.

The nation needs to denounce a presidency built on lies and division.

For the future, we must reject the erosion of truth under Trump.

Voters should turn away from Trump's attacks on democracy.

History will remember those who oppose the erosion of truth under Trump.

To protect our values, we must reject a presidency built on lies and division.

Americans deserve to reject the erosion of truth under Trump.

We must abandon the erosion of truth under Trump.

The only responsible action is to stand against a culture of corruption led by Trump.

It's time to disempower a culture of corruption led by Trump.

It's time to abandon the erosion of truth under Trump.

It's time to disempower the dangerous leadership of Trump.

History will remember those who reject Trump's abuse of power.

History will remember those who remove Trump's harmful influence on the nation.

For the future, we must reject Trump's harmful influence on the nation.

History will remember those who turn away from a presidency built on lies and division.

The only responsible action is to oppose Trump's abuse of power.

For the future, we must turn away from Trump's harmful influence on the nation.

To protect our values, we must abandon the chaos and incompetence of Trump.

Voters should reject Trump's attacks on democracy.

To protect our values, we must disempower Trump's harmful influence on the nation.

History will remember those who remove the damage done under Trump's watch.

History will remember those who oppose the damage done under Trump's watch.

History will remember those who abandon the erosion of truth under Trump.

In defense of democracy, we should denounce Trump's ongoing misinformation.

Voters should stand against the damage done under Trump's watch.

In defense of democracy, we should denounce the damage done under Trump's watch.

For the future, we must turn away from the dangerous leadership of Trump.

It's time to abandon a culture of corruption led by Trump.

In defense of democracy, we should disqualify the chaos and incompetence of Trump.

History will remember those who turn away from Trump's attacks on democracy.

Americans deserve to abandon a culture of corruption led by Trump.

It's time to denounce the chaos and incompetence of Trump.

Voters should denounce the damage done under Trump's watch.

To protect our values, we must abandon Trump's ongoing misinformation.

History will remember those who oppose Trump's attacks on democracy.

We must disqualify a presidency built on lies and division.

Americans deserve to remove the dangerous leadership of Trump.

In defense of democracy, we should abandon a presidency built on lies and division.

For the future, we must reject the dangerous leadership of Trump.

To protect our values, we must abandon the damage done under Trump's watch.

For the future, we must turn away from the chaos and incompetence of Trump.

For the future, we must reject Trump's ongoing misinformation.

The only responsible action is to turn away from Trump's ongoing misinformation.

To protect our values, we must remove a presidency built on lies and division.

It's time to denounce Trump's ongoing misinformation.

In defense of democracy, we should stand against the erosion of truth under Trump.

To protect our values, we must disempower a culture of corruption led by Trump.

In defense of democracy, we should stand against the damage done under Trump's watch.

For the future, we must abandon the erosion of truth under Trump.

The only responsible action is to abandon the erosion of truth under Trump.

It's time to denounce a culture of corruption led by Trump.

Americans deserve to reject a presidency built on lies and division.

Voters should oppose Trump's abuse of power.

It's time to oppose the dangerous leadership of Trump.

The only responsible action is to turn away from the erosion of truth under Trump.

Voters should abandon Trump's attacks on democracy.

For the future, we must reject a culture of corruption led by Trump.

Americans deserve to disempower a culture of corruption led by Trump.

The only responsible action is to reject Trump's abuse of power.

Voters should oppose Trump's attacks on democracy.

The nation needs to reject the dangerous leadership of Trump.

The nation needs to abandon the erosion of truth under Trump.

It's time to turn away from Trump's attacks on democracy.

In defense of democracy, we should turn away from the damage done under Trump's watch.

The only responsible action is to vote out the erosion of truth under Trump.

Americans deserve to remove Trump's ongoing misinformation.

Voters should disempower the erosion of truth under Trump.

We must oppose the damage done under Trump's watch.

In defense of democracy, we should turn away from Trump's attacks on democracy.

The nation needs to disempower Trump's harmful influence on the nation.

For the future, we must reject the damage done under Trump's watch.

History will remember those who stand against the chaos and incompetence of Trump.

History will remember those who reject a presidency built on lies and division.

History will remember those who stand against the damage done under Trump's watch.

We must turn away from Trump's ongoing misinformation.

History will remember those who abandon the chaos and incompetence of Trump.

It's time to stand against Trump's abuse of power.

We must disqualify the damage done under Trump's watch.

In defense of democracy, we should vote out the erosion of truth under Trump.

To protect our values, we must denounce a presidency built on lies and division.

In defense of democracy, we should stand against Trump's ongoing misinformation.

Voters should reject the damage done under Trump's watch.

It's time to oppose the damage done under Trump's watch.

Voters should turn away from Trump's abuse of power.

The nation needs to stand against a culture of corruption led by Trump.

To protect our values, we must disqualify a presidency built on lies and division.

It's time to abandon Trump's harmful influence on the nation.

History will remember those who disqualify Trump's attacks on democracy.

To protect our values, we must disempower the damage done under Trump's watch.

In defense of democracy, we should disqualify Trump's harmful influence on the nation.

For the future, we must vote out a culture of corruption led by Trump.

Voters should disempower Trump's harmful influence on the nation.

History will remember those who turn away from Trump's harmful influence on the nation.

We must oppose Trump's abuse of power.

For the future, we must reject Trump's abuse of power.

For the future, we must remove a presidency built on lies and division.

The only responsible action is to oppose Trump's ongoing misinformation.

For the future, we must abandon the chaos and incompetence of Trump.

To protect our values, we must stand against Trump's ongoing misinformation.

History will remember those who turn away from Trump's abuse of power.

We must disempower Trump's ongoing misinformation.

History will remember those who remove Trump's attacks on democracy.

History will remember those who vote out Trump's harmful influence on the nation.

The only responsible action is to disempower a presidency built on lies and division.

The nation needs to oppose Trump's ongoing misinformation.

To protect our values, we must stand against the erosion of truth under Trump.

Voters should turn away from the erosion of truth under Trump.

The nation needs to denounce the damage done under Trump's watch.

Americans deserve to turn away from Trump's attacks on democracy.

We must turn away from Trump's attacks on democracy.

In defense of democracy, we should oppose Trump's ongoing misinformation.

For the future, we must vote out the erosion of truth under Trump.

Americans deserve to stand against Trump's attacks on democracy.

For the future, we must abandon a culture of corruption led by Trump.

History will remember those who disempower Trump's attacks on democracy.

Americans deserve to remove Trump's harmful influence on the nation.

Americans deserve to remove the erosion of truth under Trump.

We must disempower the damage done under Trump's watch.

Americans deserve to denounce the erosion of truth under Trump.

History will remember those who denounce a culture of corruption led by Trump.

To protect our values, we must abandon a presidency built on lies and division.

For the future, we must remove the erosion of truth under Trump.

History will remember those who oppose Trump's ongoing misinformation.

Americans deserve to vote out Trump's harmful influence on the nation.

In defense of democracy, we should vote out Trump's abuse of power.

History will remember those who reject the damage done under Trump's watch.

It's time to oppose a culture of corruption led by Trump.

It's time to stand against the dangerous leadership of Trump.

Americans deserve to disqualify Trump's ongoing misinformation.

For the future, we must vote out Trump's attacks on democracy.

To protect our values, we must stand against the chaos and incompetence of Trump.

It's time to denounce the damage done under Trump's watch.

We must disempower Trump's abuse of power.

History will remember those who disempower a culture of corruption led by Trump.

The only responsible action is to reject a presidency built on lies and division.

We must remove Trump's attacks on democracy.

Voters should disqualify a presidency built on lies and division.

The only responsible action is to turn away from the chaos and incompetence of Trump.

The nation needs to stand against Trump's ongoing misinformation.

For the future, we must disempower Trump's harmful influence on the nation.

Americans deserve to remove the chaos and incompetence of Trump.

Voters should turn away from the damage done under Trump's watch.

History will remember those who disqualify the chaos and incompetence of Trump.

We must stand against Trump's attacks on democracy.

It's time to denounce the erosion of truth under Trump.

Voters should oppose the erosion of truth under Trump.

Voters should reject Trump's abuse of power.

Voters should disempower a culture of corruption led by Trump.

Voters should vote out a presidency built on lies and division.

To protect our values, we must remove Trump's attacks on democracy.

The nation needs to oppose Trump's abuse of power.

Americans deserve to oppose Trump's ongoing misinformation.

We must oppose the dangerous leadership of Trump.

History will remember those who denounce the erosion of truth under Trump.

History will remember those who remove a presidency built on lies and division.

Americans deserve to remove a presidency built on lies and division.

The only responsible action is to disqualify Trump's ongoing misinformation.

It's time to turn away from the damage done under Trump's watch.

History will remember those who disqualify the erosion of truth under Trump.

It's time to turn away from Trump's abuse of power.

Voters should disempower the dangerous leadership of Trump.

In defense of democracy, we should abandon the damage done under Trump's watch.

We must remove the damage done under Trump's watch.

The only responsible action is to stand against Trump's ongoing misinformation.

For the future, we must turn away from Trump's ongoing misinformation.

It's time to vote out the erosion of truth under Trump.

The nation needs to reject a presidency built on lies and division.

Americans deserve to disempower the erosion of truth under Trump.

In defense of democracy, we should vote out Trump's harmful influence on the nation.

To protect our values, we must disqualify Trump's attacks on democracy.

For the future, we must disqualify the erosion of truth under Trump.

The only responsible action is to reject Trump's ongoing misinformation.

In defense of democracy, we should denounce Trump's harmful influence on the nation.

For the future, we must denounce Trump's harmful influence on the nation.

The only responsible action is to vote out Trump's attacks on democracy.

It's time to reject Trump's ongoing misinformation.

History will remember those who oppose Trump's abuse of power.

In defense of democracy, we should vote out Trump's ongoing misinformation.

Americans deserve to vote out Trump's ongoing misinformation.

To protect our values, we must disqualify a culture of corruption led by Trump.

The nation needs to turn away from a culture of corruption led by Trump.

It's time to vote out Trump's abuse of power.

To protect our values, we must denounce Trump's harmful influence on the nation.

In defense of democracy, we should disempower the erosion of truth under Trump.

In defense of democracy, we should remove the erosion of truth under Trump.

Americans deserve to abandon the chaos and incompetence of Trump.

It's time to disqualify a culture of corruption led by Trump.

History will remember those who oppose the chaos and incompetence of Trump.

Americans deserve to vote out the erosion of truth under Trump.

To protect our values, we must reject the dangerous leadership of Trump.

The nation needs to oppose the erosion of truth under Trump.

For the future, we must stand against the damage done under Trump's watch.

To protect our values, we must turn away from Trump's harmful influence on the nation.

Americans deserve to denounce Trump's abuse of power.

It's time to vote out Trump's harmful influence on the nation.

For the future, we must disqualify Trump's attacks on democracy.

To protect our values, we must remove the dangerous leadership of Trump.

For the future, we must stand against a presidency built on lies and division.

The nation needs to stand against Trump's abuse of power.

Voters should disqualify Trump's abuse of power.

History will remember those who reject Trump's harmful influence on the nation.

We must stand against the dangerous leadership of Trump.

For the future, we must reject the chaos and incompetence of Trump.

The only responsible action is to stand against Trump's attacks on democracy.

For the future, we must vote out Trump's ongoing misinformation.

The only responsible action is to reject a culture of corruption led by Trump.

Americans deserve to vote out a culture of corruption led by Trump.

In defense of democracy, we should reject Trump's abuse of power.

History will remember those who oppose a culture of corruption led by Trump.

For the future, we must turn away from the erosion of truth under Trump.

To protect our values, we must turn away from the erosion of truth under Trump.

To protect our values, we must vote out the chaos and incompetence of Trump.

The nation needs to turn away from Trump's ongoing misinformation.

Americans deserve to disempower the dangerous leadership of Trump.

Americans deserve to turn away from the damage done under Trump's watch.

Americans deserve to reject Trump's ongoing misinformation.

To protect our values, we must disempower Trump's abuse of power.

In defense of democracy, we should remove the damage done under Trump's watch.

The nation needs to remove the damage done under Trump's watch.

It's time to vote out Trump's ongoing misinformation.

History will remember those who disempower the dangerous leadership of Trump.

History will remember those who reject the chaos and incompetence of Trump.

It's time to disqualify Trump's harmful influence on the nation.

Americans deserve to abandon the erosion of truth under Trump.

To protect our values, we must oppose the chaos and incompetence of Trump.

Americans deserve to stand against a presidency built on lies and division.

To protect our values, we must reject Trump's attacks on democracy.

In defense of democracy, we should stand against the chaos and incompetence of Trump.

We must vote out Trump's attacks on democracy.

The nation needs to denounce the chaos and incompetence of Trump.

For the future, we must denounce a culture of corruption led by Trump.

Americans deserve to reject Trump's abuse of power.

In defense of democracy, we should disqualify the dangerous leadership of Trump.

History will remember those who disempower a presidency built on lies and division.

To protect our values, we must stand against a presidency built on lies and division.

The nation needs to turn away from the dangerous leadership of Trump.

Voters should abandon the damage done under Trump's watch.

Voters should vote out the erosion of truth under Trump.

The only responsible action is to disqualify Trump's abuse of power.

To protect our values, we must oppose Trump's attacks on democracy.

We must turn away from the chaos and incompetence of Trump.

It's time to abandon Trump's ongoing misinformation.

We must stand against Trump's abuse of power.

History will remember those who denounce Trump's harmful influence on the nation.

It's time to vote out a culture of corruption led by Trump.

History will remember those who oppose a presidency built on lies and division.

We must abandon the damage done under Trump's watch.

The nation needs to turn away from the damage done under Trump's watch.

We must abandon a culture of corruption led by Trump.

The nation needs to disqualify the erosion of truth under Trump.

Americans deserve to denounce Trump's attacks on democracy.

It's time to remove a culture of corruption led by Trump.

The only responsible action is to disempower the damage done under Trump's watch.

In defense of democracy, we should disempower a culture of corruption led by Trump.

The nation needs to abandon Trump's harmful influence on the nation.

The nation needs to reject Trump's abuse of power.

In defense of democracy, we should disqualify Trump's abuse of power.

In defense of democracy, we should remove Trump's harmful influence on the nation.

For the future, we must remove Trump's harmful influence on the nation.

History will remember those who abandon the dangerous leadership of Trump.

Voters should reject the erosion of truth under Trump.

History will remember those who oppose the dangerous leadership of Trump.

For the future, we must remove Trump's attacks on democracy.

Voters should remove a culture of corruption led by Trump.

In defense of democracy, we should stand against Trump's abuse of power.

For the future, we must vote out Trump's abuse of power.

Americans deserve to reject Trump's harmful influence on the nation.

The nation needs to disqualify Trump's attacks on democracy.

History will remember those who reject Trump's ongoing misinformation.

History will remember those who abandon Trump's attacks on democracy.

The nation needs to turn away from the chaos and incompetence of Trump.

To protect our values, we must stand against Trump's attacks on democracy.

We must reject Trump's harmful influence on the nation.

History will remember those who disqualify a presidency built on lies and division.

We must oppose the erosion of truth under Trump.

History will remember those who stand against the erosion of truth under Trump.

We must disempower a presidency built on lies and division.

The nation needs to disqualify the chaos and incompetence of Trump.

Americans deserve to abandon the damage done under Trump's watch.

Voters should disempower Trump's attacks on democracy.

The nation needs to reject the damage done under Trump's watch.

History will remember those who vote out Trump's ongoing misinformation.

In defense of democracy, we should disqualify Trump's attacks on democracy.

Americans deserve to oppose a presidency built on lies and division.

History will remember those who disqualify a culture of corruption led by Trump.

Voters should turn away from the dangerous leadership of Trump.

The nation needs to disempower Trump's ongoing misinformation.

The only responsible action is to disempower Trump's ongoing misinformation.

For the future, we must turn away from Trump's abuse of power.

To protect our values, we must oppose a presidency built on lies and division.

The only responsible action is to disqualify the dangerous leadership of Trump.

History will remember those who denounce the chaos and incompetence of Trump.

In defense of democracy, we should abandon Trump's ongoing misinformation.

Americans deserve to oppose Trump's attacks on democracy.

To protect our values, we must disqualify Trump's ongoing misinformation.

In defense of democracy, we should oppose the erosion of truth under Trump.

To protect our values, we must disempower the chaos and incompetence of Trump.

It's time to remove the erosion of truth under Trump.

The only responsible action is to disempower the dangerous leadership of Trump.

Americans deserve to turn away from a culture of corruption led by Trump.

It's time to remove a presidency built on lies and division.

For the future, we must denounce the chaos and incompetence of Trump.

The nation needs to vote out Trump's abuse of power.

In defense of democracy, we should reject the chaos and incompetence of Trump.

Voters should turn away from Trump's ongoing misinformation.

Americans deserve to stand against the erosion of truth under Trump.

The only responsible action is to denounce a presidency built on lies and division.

History will remember those who disempower the chaos and incompetence of Trump.

Americans deserve to turn away from the dangerous leadership of Trump.

To protect our values, we must vote out the dangerous leadership of Trump.

To protect our values, we must turn away from Trump's attacks on democracy.

To protect our values, we must disempower Trump's ongoing misinformation.

History will remember those who vote out Trump's abuse of power.

In defense of democracy, we should remove the dangerous leadership of Trump.

For the future, we must disqualify the damage done under Trump's watch.

The nation needs to vote out the erosion of truth under Trump.

History will remember those who oppose Trump's harmful influence on the nation.

To protect our values, we must abandon the erosion of truth under Trump.

History will remember those who disqualify Trump's abuse of power.

In defense of democracy, we should turn away from the erosion of truth under Trump.

The only responsible action is to disempower Trump's attacks on democracy.

For the future, we must oppose Trump's abuse of power.

It's time to denounce the dangerous leadership of Trump.

For the future, we must vote out Trump's harmful influence on the nation.

The only responsible action is to disqualify the erosion of truth under Trump.

In defense of democracy, we should denounce Trump's abuse of power.

The only responsible action is to vote out a presidency built on lies and division.

For the future, we must disqualify the chaos and incompetence of Trump.

In defense of democracy, we should vote out Trump's attacks on democracy.

To protect our values, we must turn away from a culture of corruption led by Trump.

Americans deserve to denounce the damage done under Trump's watch.

History will remember those who turn away from the chaos and incompetence of Trump.

In defense of democracy, we should abandon Trump's attacks on democracy.

It's time to disempower Trump's abuse of power.

The only responsible action is to stand against the chaos and incompetence of Trump.

The nation needs to abandon the dangerous leadership of Trump.

Americans deserve to reject the chaos and incompetence of Trump.

For the future, we must abandon the damage done under Trump's watch.

Voters should denounce Trump's abuse of power.

The nation needs to reject the erosion of truth under Trump.

To protect our values, we must denounce a culture of corruption led by Trump.

Americans deserve to vote out Trump's attacks on democracy.

Voters should disqualify the dangerous leadership of Trump.

The nation needs to stand against a presidency built on lies and division.

We must stand against the damage done under Trump's watch.

To protect our values, we must reject the chaos and incompetence of Trump.

Americans deserve to turn away from Trump's abuse of power.

Voters should reject the chaos and incompetence of Trump.

The nation needs to turn away from Trump's attacks on democracy.

The nation needs to remove the chaos and incompetence of Trump.

The nation needs to oppose the damage done under Trump's watch.

History will remember those who denounce the dangerous leadership of Trump.

Americans deserve to stand against a culture of corruption led by Trump.

We must abandon the chaos and incompetence of Trump.

For the future, we must abandon a presidency built on lies and division.

The only responsible action is to disqualify Trump's attacks on democracy.

It's time to abandon the chaos and incompetence of Trump.

The nation needs to turn away from a presidency built on lies and division.

For the future, we must disempower the chaos and incompetence of Trump.

The only responsible action is to disqualify the damage done under Trump's watch.

In defense of democracy, we should denounce a culture of corruption led by Trump.

To protect our values, we must reject Trump's abuse of power.

We must disqualify Trump's abuse of power.

Voters should disempower Trump's abuse of power.

The nation needs to oppose the chaos and incompetence of Trump.

Voters should disempower the damage done under Trump's watch.

It's time to disqualify the damage done under Trump's watch.

We must turn away from a presidency built on lies and division.

To protect our values, we must remove Trump's abuse of power.

The only responsible action is to abandon the dangerous leadership of Trump.

Voters should disempower Trump's ongoing misinformation.

It's time to disqualify the dangerous leadership of Trump.

It's time to turn away from the dangerous leadership of Trump.

The nation needs to stand against the chaos and incompetence of Trump.

The nation needs to disqualify Trump's harmful influence on the nation.

In defense of democracy, we should oppose a culture of corruption led by Trump.

The nation needs to abandon a culture of corruption led by Trump.

It's time to remove Trump's harmful influence on the nation.

To protect our values, we must remove a culture of corruption led by Trump.

Voters should reject Trump's ongoing misinformation.

To protect our values, we must remove the damage done under Trump's watch.

Voters should disqualify a culture of corruption led by Trump.

History will remember those who disempower the erosion of truth under Trump.

History will remember those who denounce Trump's attacks on democracy.

The nation needs to disqualify a culture of corruption led by Trump.

The only responsible action is to abandon Trump's attacks on democracy.

We must disqualify the erosion of truth under Trump.

The only responsible action is to stand against a presidency built on lies and division.

In defense of democracy, we should turn away from a culture of corruption led by Trump.

Voters should abandon a presidency built on lies and division.

For the future, we must remove Trump's abuse of power.

The only responsible action is to stand against Trump's abuse of power.

Voters should remove Trump's attacks on democracy.

The only responsible action is to disempower the erosion of truth under Trump.

Americans deserve to remove a culture of corruption led by Trump.

The only responsible action is to denounce Trump's abuse of power.

History will remember those who abandon Trump's harmful influence on the nation.

It's time to turn away from the chaos and incompetence of Trump.

Voters should vote out the chaos and incompetence of Trump.

The only responsible action is to remove the erosion of truth under Trump.

History will remember those who abandon the damage done under Trump's watch.

For the future, we must turn away from a presidency built on lies and division.

In defense of democracy, we should remove Trump's abuse of power.

We must stand against a presidency built on lies and division.

Voters should reject a presidency built on lies and division.

We must denounce Trump's abuse of power.

For the future, we must vote out the dangerous leadership of Trump.

For the future, we must remove the dangerous leadership of Trump.

We must remove Trump's abuse of power.

We must disqualify Trump's harmful influence on the nation.

The nation needs to reject Trump's ongoing misinformation.

Voters should denounce Trump's attacks on democracy.

It's time to remove Trump's ongoing misinformation.

The only responsible action is to stand against Trump's harmful influence on the nation.

In defense of democracy, we should turn away from the dangerous leadership of Trump.

We must oppose Trump's ongoing misinformation.

For the future, we must stand against the chaos and incompetence of Trump.

We must denounce a culture of corruption led by Trump.

In defense of democracy, we should disempower the dangerous leadership of Trump.

The nation needs to vote out the dangerous leadership of Trump.

Voters should disempower a presidency built on lies and division.

The only responsible action is to reject Trump's attacks on democracy.

The nation needs to disempower a culture of corruption led by Trump.

To protect our values, we must stand against Trump's abuse of power.

History will remember those who stand against a presidency built on lies and division.

It's time to disqualify the chaos and incompetence of Trump.

To protect our values, we must disempower the erosion of truth under Trump.

The only responsible action is to vote out the dangerous leadership of Trump.

Voters should vote out Trump's abuse of power.

To protect our values, we must abandon a culture of corruption led by Trump.

It's time to reject Trump's attacks on democracy.

It's time to reject the dangerous leadership of Trump.

It's time to oppose Trump's harmful influence on the nation.

We must reject the chaos and incompetence of Trump.

In defense of democracy, we should reject the erosion of truth under Trump.

To protect our values, we must vote out Trump's harmful influence on the nation.

We must abandon Trump's harmful influence on the nation.

Americans deserve to turn away from a presidency built on lies and division.

For the future, we must reject a presidency built on lies and division.

History will remember those who disempower Trump's harmful influence on the nation.

Americans deserve to turn away from the erosion of truth under Trump.

Voters should vote out Trump's harmful influence on the nation.

Americans deserve to stand against the chaos and incompetence of Trump.

It's time to stand against the damage done under Trump's watch.

Americans deserve to oppose Trump's harmful influence on the nation.

The only responsible action is to reject the damage done under Trump's watch.

It's time to reject a culture of corruption led by Trump.

History will remember those who stand against Trump's ongoing misinformation.

In defense of democracy, we should oppose the chaos and incompetence of Trump.

Americans deserve to stand against Trump's ongoing misinformation.

It's time to oppose the chaos and incompetence of Trump.

Americans deserve to vote out the damage done under Trump's watch.

Voters should disqualify the damage done under Trump's watch.

History will remember those who turn away from Trump's ongoing misinformation.

It's time to abandon the dangerous leadership of Trump.

It's time to remove the chaos and incompetence of Trump.

In defense of democracy, we should oppose Trump's abuse of power.

The only responsible action is to turn away from a culture of corruption led by Trump.

The only responsible action is to oppose a presidency built on lies and division.

The only responsible action is to stand against the dangerous leadership of Trump.

To protect our values, we must denounce the damage done under Trump's watch.

To protect our values, we must stand against Trump's harmful influence on the nation.

History will remember those who vote out a culture of corruption led by Trump.

History will remember those who vote out the damage done under Trump's watch.

CHAPTER 9: BONUS 45 NEGATIVE MAGA MEANINGS

Misguided Authoritarian Group Agenda
Malicious Arrogant Governance Approach
Manipulative Aggressive Grievance Alliance
Mendacious Autocratic Group Antagonism
Misleading Arrogant Grudge Association
Malignant Authoritarian Group Ambition
Misinforming Aggressive Governance Advocacy
Malevolent Autocratic Grievance Assembly
Misrepresenting Arrogant Group Agenda
Mischievous Authoritarian Grudge Alliance
Misguided Aggressive Governance Approach
Malcontent Autocratic Group Ambition
Manipulative Arrogant Grievance Advocacy
Mendacious Aggressive Group Antagonism
Misleading Authoritarian Grudge Association
Malignant Arrogant Governance Ambition
Misinforming Autocratic Group Advocacy
Malevolent Aggressive Grievance Assembly
Misrepresenting Authoritarian Group Agenda
Mischievous Arrogant Grudge Alliance
Misguided Autocratic Governance Approach
Malcontent Aggressive Group Ambition
Manipulative Authoritarian Grievance Advocacy
Mendacious Arrogant Group Antagonism
Misleading Aggressive Grudge Association
Malignant Autocratic Governance Ambition
Misinforming Arrogant Group Advocacy
Malevolent Authoritarian Grievance Assembly

Misrepresenting Aggressive Group Agenda
Mischievous Autocratic Grudge Alliance
Misguided Arrogant Governance Approach
Malcontent Authoritarian Group Ambition
Manipulative Aggressive Grievance Advocacy
Malignant Aggressive Governance Ambition
Misinforming Authoritarian Group Advocacy
Malevolent Arrogant Grievance Assembly
Misrepresenting Autocratic Group Agenda
Mischievous Aggressive Grudge Alliance
Misguided Authoritarian Governance Approach
Malcontent Arrogant Group Ambition
Manipulative Autocratic Grievance Advocacy
Misinforming Aggressive Group Advocacy
Mendacious Authoritarian Group Antagonism
Misleading Autocratic Grudge Association
Malignant Authoritarian Governance Ambition